WRITING WORK

A Collection of Poems by Poets
of the Southern San Joaquin Valley

in collaboration with

The Walter Stiern Library,

The School of Arts and Humanities,

The English Department

at

California State University, Bakersfield

2017

Many thanks to Curt Asher and Kristi Chavez at the Walter Stiern Library and Liora Gubkin at the School of Arts & Humanities for their ongoing enthusiasm and support of poetry.

Previous issues of the "Writing" series can be found in the Walter Stiern Library collection at California State University, Bakersfield.

Writing Work (2017)
Writing the Drought (2016)

Edited by Matthew Woodman

Cover Photograph, "A Construction of Humanity," by Madison Tingey

Copyright © 2017

All rights reserved. No part of this collection may be reproduced or transmitted in any form or by any means, electronic or mechanical, including photocopying and recording, without the respective author's expressed written permission.

WELCOME

In 1991, his penultimate year teaching for Fresno State, Philip Levine won the National Book Award for his collection of poems *What Work Is*, the title poem of which contains the lines

> You know what work is—if you're
> old enough to read this you know what
> work is, although you may not do it.
> Forget you [...]

and pivots from being an anti-capitalist critique about waiting in an employment line to arguing that the truest "work" is the act of expressing one's love in the form of *philia* (friendship and goodwill) or *agape* (charity and altruism). This sudden unexpected shift is reminiscent of how D.H. Lawrence's poem "Whatever Man Makes" also defamiliarizes the subject (and object) of work:

> Whatever man makes and makes it live
> lives because of the life put into it.
> A yard of India muslin is alive with Hindu life.
> And a Navajo woman, weaving her rug in the pattern of her dream
> must run the pattern out in a little break at the end
> so that her soul can come out, back to her.
>
> But in the odd pattern, like snake marks on the sand
> it leaves its trail.

Too often, we feel ourselves to be working like dogs (for peanuts), trapped on the hamster wheel (in the rat race), chasing the carrot (or karat) as just another cog in the machine. The poems that follow are denunciations and celebrations, interrogations and denials, prosecutions and defenses. We'll leave it to the reader to follow the trail, to answer Levine's question as to what work is . . .

CONTENTS

Greg Bolanos — Self Improvement / Animal Corp.

Annis Cassells — Miss Holley, Biology II / Visiting Hours

Portia Choi — Blower / Bouquet

Sunnee Crider — Blue Collar Dad

Priti Devaprakash — On the Dualities of Our Lives / Instrument of Mass Injection

Erika Diaz — Controller / *Sufrimiento*

Jeff Eagan — Bullseye's Mascots: The Smart, the Sad, the Dull, and Wasted or Kingsmere Moondoggie's Legacy

Shelley Evans — Thinking about Work, a Bad Hair Day / Work, Work, Work

Jack Hernandez — Buddha in Detroit / Sluggards and Ants

Anke Hodenpijl — being Her / Work

Catherine Abbey Hodges — Intro to Lit / Ash Wednesday Morning

Anthony Jauregui — Work is: / Diary of an Uber Driver

Emily Johnston — The Binder / What Work Is

David Kettler — Carrying Weight / Hard Work

Mateo Lara — A Working Flame / On Working Towards Goals and Love

Rose Lester — Good Therapy / Wax Paper Hands

Marit MacArthur — A Calling

Shaina Rae Panga	Deposit
	Both Dressed in White
Chyna Parker	Lumpenproletariat
	Schumpeter's Gale
Shelby Pinkham	Do You Want to Send the Message Without Any Subject?
Nashwa Rafiq	Writing Scars
	In the Red
Diana Ramirez	Repeated Effort
	Work Shines
Bailey Russell	A Cold Morn'
	Godspeed for Your Work Begun
Sidney Russell	Scritch, Scratch
	Toiling, Toiling
Mark Saso	To My Hard Working Father
	Dirty Work
Don Thompson	Condors
	Yard Work
Tim Vivian	On These Streets
	When Memory We Inspect
Jana Lee Wong	A Teacher's Work
	A Docent's Work
Matthew Woodman	Purchase (Your Own Title)
	Workers' Rhythm

Self Improvement

What matters most is not
Material gain, people aren't objects
Yet they collect dust all the same.
Focus your efforts on those worth polishing,
Those who aren't thinking of demolishing
Everything you built when times weren't rough.
Focus on the people who don't act tough.

Well... Person, I should say. Me, myself, and I should say
There really is no other way
Because you can't leave you
No matter how hard you try,
Unless of course you want to die
But even then you're stuck with you

Friends can say all day they'll come through,
Believe them if you think them true,
But only you really know you.

Only you can make that difference.
Self love is not a privilege.
It's knowing you're better than what you've been through,
Because you're the realest one
When all you have is you.

--Greg Bolanos

Animal Corp.

Horrendous hay bales
Stacked a mile high, breaking backs
With unflinching eye.

Gratuitous grapes
Plucked from the vine, stealing sweat
For a salty brine.

Capricious cotton
Pricking the hand, history
Made ugly demands.

All the kings horses
Thought themselves content, being
Ridden till the end.

Never knowing the
Cumshaw of heightened living,
The warmth of the boot
Was more than fitting; Boxer
Died unthinking. Unwitting.

--Greg Bolanos

Miss Holley,
    Biology II

Deep, dark eyes, fire-lit coals
set in her shiny brown face
peered over half-frame glasses.
How can you tell
a male tortoise from a female?

Miss Holley waited.
Silence.   Eternity.
The male has long toenails
so he can hold on
during cop-u-lation.

Even white teeth flashed
her smile wide, full-lipped.
A few caught on, tittered
while some shot furtive glances,
or sought clarity or looked away.

Day One.
She copped our attention.

Her work was pure love,
love of teaching and learning
love of guiding, inspiring
work infused with passion.
Her expectations towered,
ensuring we could not fail
to outgrow ourselves
to become more.

And Miss Holley was more.
More than my teacher
she embodied possibility,
mentored this young girl.

Our faces
my dreams
her memories
reflecting in each other.

--Annis Cassells

Visiting Hours

Crowding at the nursery window
fathers, aunts & uncles, grandparents cluck and grin
at a gaggle of first-borns, middle kids and after-thoughts
ravenous, eager to smack at rubber nipples
or suckle at their mothers' breasts.

Minutes before these angels of torture
pulsed and pressed to breathe air,
pushing grown women into hard labor
arduous as working on a chain gang .
Imprisoned, they strained towards freedom,
rushed headlong into the light.

Crowding at the nursery window,
Look at that head full of curly hair.
There's ours, the cutest one here.
How smart she is already.
He looks just like his daddy.

Crowding at the nursery window,
joy   pride   wonder
Lavish congratulations.
Scant consideration
of the wearied women on the ward.

--Annis Cassells

Blower

A Guatemalan young man dreams of his baby,
hunched over by the heaviness of a blower-back-pack,
aims the nozzle at the clipped grass and crumbling leaves.

The long-sleeved shirt and hat-flaps cover his ears
protecting the skin from the searing sun:
reddening and blistering.

Bakersfield heat cracks the lips, parches the throat.
The blown dust seeps into the crevices of the skin,
spores of death lodge in the lung sacs.

Labor to feed a child, at home
hundreds of miles away.
Dust and sweat sting the tearless eyes.

--Portia Choi

Bouquet

A concrete, rectangular building. A health clinic, not a prison. Windows placed ten feet high—hard to break—some light shining in.

A clinic for persons with lung disease.

I sat at a desk, near an examining table and x-ray view boxes.

The door opened fast. A man in baggy pants and ruffled hair shouted "F- - - you, Jap." His eyes glaring suspiciously for a moment, then he slammed the door. A stench of sweat and urine lingered in the room.

I learned that he was on supervised treatment, a treatment where a person is given an injection and watched swallowing the pills. Even with his schizophrenia and being without a home, he came to clinic, regularly, for his treatments.

About two years later, I saw him at the clinic.

He was shaven, hair combed, clothes clean. He had a bouquet of red roses, daisies and leaves in his right hand.

I said, with a smile, "How beautiful."

"From my garden," he said.

Later that day, I saw the bouquet in a jar on the nurse's desk.

She was the nurse who had treated the man, giving him the shots and watching him swallow his medication.

I said to the nurse, "How beautiful."

"From the neighbor's garden, probably," she said. Not looking up, she continued to write in a chart.

--Portia Choi

Blue Collar Dad

He wakes in the morning
with the turn of his head.
No alarm clock goes off
but he gets out of bed.

The smell of aftershave lingers
as his kisses his wife.
He heads out the door
as the day comes to life.

Sweat covers his brow
before the sun hits its high
he hurries through lunch
but the hours tick by.

He gets home and his
babies, they come running.
Saying hi, begging for time,
their smiles are stunning.

They stay out and play
as he tends to the lawn.
This job he'd do
from dusk till dawn.

--Sunnee Crider

On The Dualities of Our Lives

One man's pain
Is another man's pleasure
Just as one man's toil
Is another man's treasure
One man's grind
Is another man's gratification
Just as one man's drudge
Is another man's diversion
And so it is
With each of our lives
One man succumbs
While the other survives

--Priti Devaprakash

Instrument of Mass Injection

Monday morning
Just sitting in a drawer
Darkness all around
How long it has been since I saw the light of day
How I long to do something rather than just sit here
Useless, firmly capped
Packed in with my neighbors like cats in a box
Suddenly a thin crack of light starts to appear
I see a gloved hand with ghostly outstretched fingers reaching for me
Maybe she will make me useful today
Finally, my time has come
Today I fulfill my purpose
Does she know how to use me correctly?
She should really hold me further away from the bench
Considering how dirty it is
Down we go to the vivarium
The darkness is flooded with fluorescent light as the switch is flipped
Mice scurrying apprehensively in their cages
She is removing the orange cap that protects my sharp, sterile eye
I feel the cold solution being drawn into my very heart
A mouse grabbed by its neck is squealing in protest
She is turning it upside down
I can't stand the anticipation
Ah, it has arrived
In one swift motion my sharp tip plunges under the abdominal skin of the mouse
A sharp squeal, a drop of blood, and it is over
And so it goes

--Priti Devaprakash

Controller

Clock ticking, counting out each hour in my head
Feels like an eternity that is lethal to the dead
Standing, checking in, checking out
This job is a nightmare
A haziness that makes you blurt out in prayer
I have lost all sensation of the mind
Oh yes, in definite need of a tall glass of wine
Is this crap over yet?
I think I have done enough

Ring! Ring!
"How may I help you?"
One by One
Jesus come down yourself and help me out
"She can take the next guest."
Can I please take a rest?

Friday finally hits and I can close my eyes and sleep
Not really... Just kidding.
Wake up your shift is coming up
Get dressed, work, and repeat
Wait, is it lunch so I can eat

I pass the toy aisle and I hear a slight whisper to my left ear
What is that I hear?
The teddy bears murmured as if they were speaking to me
It said, "How are you today my dear, you seem a little down?"
I thought I was hallucinating.
Were these just voices in my head that wanted me to look like a clown?

I ignored it all, I walked away
Then I realized my shift was almost over for the day
I still had my daily goal to reach, I fell into my slump once again
I felt distraught, as if I was going to fall down to the ground into black hole
"Wait one minute!"
The cashier box said, "Set up your game unless you want someone to take
        your place."
"You have to really want this; you must be in it to win the game"
How bad do you want to be flame?

--Erika Diaz

Sufrimiento

Physically and mentally drained
That is what I am.
You sense you are on the right path
But you're completely off course
Why is this happening?
Why is that happening?
Tell me god I plead to you
I'm on my knees I'm begging you
Make it stop!
I do not deserve such pain and neither does he
Overworked, I tell him everyday
Does he listen? Absolutely!... Not.
Stubborn as can be, I wonder where I get it from
Oh father of mine, I realize no one is perfect
I really do.
I only ask you one thing, listen closely
Open up your ears as well as your mind
You are imbalanced, not well
The time is ticking down now

--Erika Diaz

Bullseye's Mascots: The Smart, the Sad, the Dull, and Wasted
or Kingsmere Moondoggie's Legacy

Ricky: smart guy, former med school student, doesn't like "guests," works in stockroom, ACTIVE

Charles (Chuck): biker, bad ass, Minnesota native, handles the rowdy teenagers and belligerent "guests," best fake smile, ETL Hard Lines, TRANSFERRED

Shane: slick dude, manager, rich parents, husky, married twice, one kid, a worldly man, laid-back, likes to party, TERMINATED

"Lazy" Stacy: diminutive, Ed Helms obsessive, resident pseudo-intellectual elitist, self-proclaimed expert on all things "nerdy," sings and dances badly-out loud, corner cutter, alcoholic, VOLUNTARILY TERMINATED

Cindy: high-pitched Arkie twang, a "no one can be this happy" smile, bleached blond Texas bouffant, mother to all-biological mother to nine rascals, Redcard© application record holder 2010-2013, best banana and mayonnaise sandwich maker, RESIGNED

Yessica: teenage mom, kids with mild lead poisoning from Vallarta popsicles, sometime student, hard worker, open mind, still blending Starbucks Frappucinos©, ACTIVE

Connie: big ginger, waist-length braided ponytail, broken back, busted knees, works three jobs, EBT cardholder, perpetual glasses on forehead, still asking "Would you like to save 5% today with a Redcard©?", ACTIVE

Aaron, a blast from the high school past, skinny club soccer kid turned muscular corporate dingo, pasty freckled face, overly confident hand-shaker and back-slapper, receding hairline, loves Goldschläger, Store Manager, TRANSFERRED

--Jeff Eagan

Thinking about Work, a Bad Hair Day

Thinking of the four-letter word "work," the first thing that comes to mind
Is that the job should be a little fun to balance the daily grind.
If you can't have some enjoyment while at your job all week,
Soon it might become drudgery and the future may look bleak.

From 9 to 5 if you must sit behind a desk at work,
Without a little humor your duties you might shirk.
If the task has become boring, you might feel ineffective.
These ideas on workmanship should give you some perspective.

"Another day, another dollar." "Rome wasn't built in a day."
"Man cannot live by bread alone." - common quotes that people say.
Conan O'Brien said, "Work hard and amazing things will happen."
"I have not failed, just found 10,000 ways that don't work," Edison.

"Choose a job you love, and you'll never have to work a day in your life."
Those are words from Confucius; and Bette Davis said, "I work to stay
 alive."
A quote from Satchel Paige is, "Work like you don't need the money."
"Let the beauty of what you love be what you do," stated Rumi.

"Chop your own wood; it will warm you twice," said Mack King.
"He that waits on fortune is never sure of dinner," Ben Franklin.
Elbert Hubbard once said, "We work to become, not to acquire."
"Every noble work is at first impossible," Thomas Carlyle.

Sophocles was known to say, "Without labor nothing prospers."
"Nobody ever drowned in his own sweat," a quote by Ann Landers.
Gordon Hinckley said, "Without hard work nothing grows but weeds."
"The only place success comes before work ... the dictionary," Lombardi's.

Buddha said, "Work out your own salvation. Do not depend on others."
"Men for the sake of getting a living forget to live," quote of Margaret
 Fuller's.
"Opportunity is missed by most people because it is dressed in
Overalls and looks like work," said Thomas Edison.

Thomas Dekker stated, "Honest labor bears a lovely face."
"To be a poet is a condition not a profession," Robert Frost.
Which leads me to profess the thing that truly makes a difference:
Employees with a strong work ethic earn respect and reverence.

Criss Jami said, "A good work ethic is not so much a concern
For hard work but rather one for responsibility," – an upturn.
"When you master the art of work, then your life becomes a work of art."
A quote by Sotero Lopez, II, which should be taken to heart.

Andrena Sawyer said, "Whatever you do, be sure to do it well."
Per Halberstam, "…it was not so much for a promotion as to excel…."
Janna Cachola stated that "Professionalism … should be defined by a
       person's work ethic."
T. Nagao said, "A bad hair day is not a good excuse for calling in sick."

--Shelley J. Evans

Work, Work, Work

Work, work, work…
Work my life away
Nine to five, stay alive
Monday through Friday

Hurray for the weekend
When I get to spend
Good quality time
On nobody's dime
Relaxing at home
Writing a poem
Reading a book
I may even cook

Then Sunday's done and
I do it all again

--Shelley J. Evans

Buddha in Detroit

Outside my gated
Grosse Pointe community
as I drove my father's
Porsche, I saw a toothless
woman trolling for garbage
scattered wantonly on a street
denuded of trees   concrete
scarred   potholed   hard
like the three men strutting
their force before the weak.

The smelly torn cloak
of run-down suffering
covered me, made me
leave home to wander
among the blind
broken houses
of Detroit's ruined body.

I sat beneath the fractured shadow
of an abandoned auto factory
realized only selfless
hearts water life,
heard laughter
from the three
pause   empty
when I opened
my hands.

--Jack Hernandez

Sluggards and Ants

Go to the ant, you sluggard,
          see its ways and get wisdom.
                  (Proverbs 6:6)

There's a lesson here:
The ant gets the house,
car, girl, and praise
from other ants, bees, worms
who march, fly straight, and dig
through the passing of daily time.
The sluggard pitied, occasionally
reviled as morally slack,
gets only the odd, surprising
detour, the scent of flowers
lounged upon, and the feel
of lazing in wet, cool earth.

--Jack Hernandez

being Her

used to be her deficiency
became her necessity
became her hope
became her Legacy
became her Opus
became our Our Birthright

we dance with Her descant
disremembering
the cheerless and sticky rejection
the pluck of her pushback
the rumpus of Her March
as she labored for
equal rights
equal pay
equal humanity

as we claim our apologue
from her swindle sheet
we exhume the after birth
and the caterwaul of resistance
to the unjust reincarnation
of the Philistine Shadow
rising like stench from a too shallow grave

Are we to be ransomed again?

And

What is the price for the uncaging of life without fear?
When will we be able to fly with the quiet confidence of a flock
murmurating in unison
agreeing through unconscious heart
that we are full-toned, muscled and mighty?

Is it true, what they say?

A Woman's Work is never done.

being Her

sure feels that way.

--Anke Hodenpijl

Work

that place in between
between imagination and satisfaction
between prayer and holiness
between spirit and love
between birth and re-birth.

Gratitude is the dough I knead
with intentional hands
shaping and
caring for
that place in between
once again
retelling
this time with potent iterations
full-flavored, unconfused and knowing
Truth ages with time.

Today, in my older years,
my Work is louder
because the ears of others
have forgotten.
Or maybe they did not get
the text,
the instant message or
the tweet.

Let my work begin afresh,
rising,
not hesitatingly like a distant sunrise,
but rather like an eruption,
unwilling to be punched down,
here
now
I say

My pussy is not yours to grab!
Your alternative facts, are not my reality.
My memory is clear.
Your words. Can. Not. reconstruct Herstory.

my Suffrage Brogue
creates an unmistakable landscape
as surely as the molten lava
claims the mountain and the sea
from the center
to the

this is who I am
this is where I've been

and,   Yes,   THIS is still my work.

--Anke Hodenpijl

Intro to Lit

I got no use for words
said Bill's dad a long time
before the summer Bill was my student,
but those are words that stay
with you a long time.

That summer the bees began to go missing.
Ernie, who most days sat in front of Bill,
said he didn't much mind.
I got no use for bees said Ernie, said
on a sweaty break

between simile and metaphor
that as a kid in Modesto he'd been stung all over
by a swarm of bees another boy
had knocked out of a tree.
All over my face and arms, my bare stomach.

That was the day Bill told me
on the way to the parking lot
what his dad had said. *But I needed his words*
Bill said. *I sure's hell had a use for them.*
Asphalt mirage-pools

shimmered with students, poplars,
pick-ups. Bill said Ernie's bees
made him want to cry like a good poem.
Like this he said, surprised, touching
his face. *Like this right now.*

--Catherine Abbey Hodges
From *Instead of Sadness*, Gunpowder Press, 2015

Ash Wednesday Morning

The fat candle in the kitchen window burns down
like a rose spilling open. We light a scrap of paper
from the flame, and with the ashes, a little olive oil,
cross each other's foreheads. Margo's in the hospital
again. I stop to see her on my way to school,
go straight from there to class. My students have come
from their night shifts at the nursing home
and Wal-Mart, from Mass, from dropping off the baby
at daycare. They shuffle pages, share staplers.
We look into each other's faces as they hand me their essays.
Who knows how long we've got inside these dusty skins.
We're burning down together, ashes mingling already.

--Catherine Abbey Hodges
From *Instead of Sadness*, Gunpowder Press, 2015

Work Is:

Lacing an orange-yellow pair of Timbaland, ankle high, skin tight

Making anonymous phone calls, making a victim say yes, stealing an identity

Pretending to love a 56 year old predator for a crisp Lincoln on your bare ass, wearing a bustier

Wrapping a Breitbart tech editor's best-selling novel at a Barnes and Noble during Christmas

Forcing an 11 year old black kid wearing Filas to sell your skunk weed on MLK Blvd

Not using punctuation in a Facebook post to avoid sounding pretentious

Giving a compliment to someone that doesn't deserve it

Taping your tits down so your double XL shirt fits right

Inviting the lunatic loner in the group to a party so they don't kill themselves

Taking a class in Gender/Literature/Film/Society

Delivering a pizza to the ghetto side of town

Wrongly prescribing an opioid addict with Fentanyl for lower lumbar pain

Standing outside a department store holding a sign that says your hungry, hurting, stuck

Work is more than blistered hands, long hours, fry cooks, and field workers.

Work ranges from 2 seconds to 78 hours a week.

Work is a gear turning, moaning, and creaking in your brain. Work is a FitBit that reads: 45 CAL/Hr.

Work is burning calories, maybe that's why I don't like exercising.

--Anthony Juaregui

Diary of an Uber Driver

As I was changing out the compact disc in my car last Thursday:

The *Buzzcocks "Orgasm Addict"* had just about :03 seconds left on the timer; not yet finished.

I wanted to freshen up the cacophony of sounds in my car and in an attempt to do so I grabbed the CD case in the seat behind me; almost there.

A woman I've got emotionally strung around my fingertips sits behind me; never fucked.

The chicken nuggets on the passenger seat floor; never eaten.

All of this happened just before I hit the car in front of me; finished.

I could live in this moment forever; the pre-crash.

Exist in the pre-climax; forever.

So why don't I?

Coming is hard,

But I really wanna crash.

Part 2: Diary of an Uber Passenger

It's 7:56. I'm gonna be late again.

Slow down. We're gonna crash.

SLOW crash.

8:01. I'm late. Fired.

--Anthony Juaregui

The Binder

Why must I be here?
Why must these things be inside me?
Why do you need to be in here?
I guess it's better to be out here
Then to be shoved back in there

It's just another Monday
And we are here again
Spread out all over the table
Just waiting
For opening night to begin

She opens me up
And slams my face onto the table
The weight of the papers
Presses into my back
I feel so unstable

Do we really need this entire script?
Does anybody really care about the second act?
Why don't we simply move pages 280 to 394?
It would relieve the pressure on my back.
Honestly, why can't things be simple with you?

I know you're tired
We can't kill the actors right now
 Just be patient
Wait until after the show
I'm tired too but
My only purpose in life
Is to grow.
So, take a deep breath
And get on with the show.

--Emily Johnston

What Work Is

I'm tired
I'm just going to say it
I'm tired of doing this
I'm tired of doing that
Why am I being nice for?
Fuck this,
Fuck that,
And overall, Fuck you!
It was fun in the beginning but
Honestly now I just don't give a crap
I put hours of none stop labor into
this laughing factory
For what?
I don't get a paycheck
I don't even get an ounce of respect
No, what I get is to be everyone's mother
When I hate children
Play for a team
But somehow I'm the mascot, cheerleader and
The quarterback
Be the one everyone goes to
But find somebody fucking else
I'm tired
With blood and bruises on my hands
Sweat in my eyes
The only thing in life I'm working for
Is my sweat demise.

--Emily Johnston

Carrying Weight

I'm feelin tired and broken
My hand stuck to the plough
I'd love to take a rest
I somehow don't know how

Been carrying a lot of weight
I feel it in my bones
Waiting for an open gate
Maybe I threw too many stones

The sunrise starts my day
Nighttime draws the shades
The weeks all seem the same
Enthusiasm fades

I drink my cup of Joe
Knowin I gotta roll
Keep goin with the flow
Till the goin takes its toll

The missus, she goes too
And it's oh, so hard to see
The wheel is spinnin free
And the hamster it is me

I see my feet a runnin
And the wheel is really spinnin
I think I'm gaining ground
But the wheel just keeps on winnin

Been working since a youngin
And I see no other way
Rest will someday come
When in the ground I lay

-- David Kettler

Hard Work

I work like a dog in the Bakersfield heat
There's a pain in my back and a hurt in my seat

My legs they are sore and my feet they are numb
And that pound in my head like the beat of a drum

The good book it says that a man who won't work
Well he shouldn't even eat … that old lazy jerk

Not word for word but the meaning you get
You work for your keep and your family is set

I really don't mind doing my part
But it seems really dark the earlier I start

And when I finish the sun has gone down
The street lights already are painting the town

The days they all melt into fatigable one
My work never finished the job never done

When my sore body at last hits the hay
The pain in my shoulder just might go away

I'm so excited my head it will spin
Because tomorrow morning I start all again!

--David Kettler

A Working Flame

Transmutation—existed in parallel space,
And my grandfather resurrected,
And we were working toward a flame, salvation.

I survived two times that day, sultry and sadistic,
Never worried about currency vibrating in my pockets,
I let it wild and I was loved, reborn in sentimental ashes.

I'm assisting myself—found perfection in routine,
Fantasy drifting against industrial identities,
Pulsing in red, burning down our royal need.

And the simmering is a dream of M and who he is pursuing,
Down and out in the south,
On the prowl for moonlight and flesh worthy of his touch,
I work toward a pivotal moment of new names, flames upon the church of my love,
On gold and silver and glass,
I tempt a world toward progression,
And ask for nothing back, but eyes,
And the hum in my body that never gives up,
that works itself out in its infernal mood.

--Mateo Lara

On Working Towards Goals and Love

For Mark S.

A simple aspiration, precious goals—engraved onto bones,
Beating back your parent's droning, beating back excessive talking, your soul's excessive use,
Living the dream against the heat of a day, new tethered currents between people,
Little green dots flashing from phones, working toward carnal domes, experience beyond "Here."

                        I have reconciled with you time and time again,
                    Meant to work out tattered and frayed edges of friendships,
                    Overrun with other people's love that is not ours,
           As if we are teaching ourselves the fundamentals to truth and caring,
    Stuck in Atlanta, stuck in Zabok, stuck in ravaged lands of wanting more
                                      but never having enough,
                            And I look back and remember:
You're going to be a teacher, travel, disappear, like this, one more year. one
                                                more year?

There's one notion: what will I work towards?
You say I think too much, as if projecting severed/churning machines,
Losing too much in our economy, I would ask you to hold me,
But I am Dow and Down and rushing for approval from too many people and places,
And things, I wish you'd sweep into me, but you'd only say: work harder.

  I work against changing times, and changing climates, against our weather,
  Our political waves rushing and finding me successful, or distressed against
      your approaching departure from this working hand, working to know,
  Working to know as much as you do…because you're right…love…you're
  right, I've got a long way to go, in an echo carved deeply as if an empty sea
                                            were swirling inside me.

--Mateo Lara

Good Therapy

Good therapy begins with the lightest touch,
A warm welcome,
a smile,
A comfortable chair,
Lighting soft and inviting,
A deep and steady breath.
A focused, yet gentle gaze.
Gradually a softening,
Breaking down of barriers,
Breaking through old encrustations.
A heartfelt connection
The tangled ball of string
That is the self
Is explored,
Untangled.
An innocent question, a curiosity,
A comment, an image,
And blessed silence.
Suddenly the room fills with light.
Insight flashes,
Hot and fast
Urging you forward
Beyond where you've gone before.
Yes, Good therapy begins with the lightest touch.

--Rose Lester

Wax Paper Hands

Wax-paper hands
Skin worn thin
As if one more washing
might wear them away
No longer rough.
No soil under the fingernails
No heavy grease stained crevices
That no amount of washing could remove.
No longer calloused from hard work.
    Digging in the garden,
        Repairing the tractor
            Writing letters,
Or waving good bye from the driveway.
Wax-paper hands,
Resting on a chest,
    white,
        clean,
            soft
Still at last.

--Rose Lester

A Calling

Finding one
ought to feel like sudden
freedom,
as when what was
last night
a wall of snow
this afternoon
is pouring, spraying,
streaming down
the cliff face.

Abruptly shown the way
by the thoughtless sun
burning away clouds,
trapped particles
that vibrated in crystal
formations of cold
hard-working boredom
all winter long
suddenly discover
how fast they can move
under the right conditions.

Spring is a new job
the ice water prefers,
taking on the shape
of the rocks it spills over,
taking it off
and slipping away.

--Marit MacArthur

Deposit

Dark and cool
Alone
A small, lit square
From which a shadowy figure emerges
Some sort of opening
Where the small, lit square was.

Something has stepped into me…
Wait!
Isn't this Saturday morning?

Alone
With a sweet gift
Of truffle clinging to my innards.
Not that bad.

Again, a small, lit square
The same shadowy figure coming from it.
Stepping into me…
My purpose in this world?
To receive gifts.

Again, alone –
But beer this time.
Golden liquid coursed my insides;
The smell so strong like urine's.
What others would give the stink-eye,
Is normal for me.

Afternoon
So many creatures come to me, in me,
Leaving me gifts.
I'm full and intoxicated…
Satisfied
Reeking sweet and sour

A large, lit rectangle
A huge shadowy figure
Flicks on the lights and stares
What are you looking at?
Why don't you follow the instructions?

--Shaina Rae Panga

Both Dressed in White

Saline drip
He rides the waves
He searches for her
Protect
Love

Shellback
She checks the charts
She waits for him
Heal
Love

Unconditional Surrender
Seven years in wedded bliss
"Hello, baby girl!"
Work hard
Love

--Shaina Rae Panga

Lumpenproletariat

Don't wait for the headlights
To peak in the window
I'll trickle in -
Piece by peace

Don't wait for the
Boom or bust of our
Deflated car to jostle your
Inflated chest

Don't listen to our neighbors
And their General Glut
They understand little of
Dreams and dirt

Don't kiss me goodbye
In the morning
I've got Say's law
To keep it laissez-faire

Don't hold me when I sob
They pay me to be
The gross domestic product
Of a working class job

--Chyna Parker

Schumpeter's Gale

Do not listen to the
Moans of broken men
We've got permanent
Domicile on their backs

Do not underestimate
Our caste to separate
Brown v. Board
With another iron curtain

Do not bring us to court
We've got our hands
In pockets you've
Sewn and stitched.

Do not march or sing
We've got our boots
On your mother's neck
To keep you civil.

Do not fight and protest
Our executive authority
Governs your
Ten cent thoughts

Do not dream too big
Our creative destruction
Is a means to an end of
Your petty function.

--Chyna Parker

Do You Want to Send the Message Without Any Subject?

I have been too busy working to write about work.
And I have been too depressed to write about work.
I am not sure which of these things actually prevented me from writing any
      poetry about work.

But I have been avoiding myself.

My mother sent me this text message:
With the new revelation of fake news and bad journalists,
Maybe you should consider journalism.
Feb 28 10:59 AM

I avoided texting her back.

I have been working at being happy
I can't seem to write and be happy.
Also I really don't want anyone reading my thoughts or opinions right now.
I know that's part of the depression.
But I am worried that someone will read them
And call me out.

Because I hate my dad and my sister.
Because I hate my manager and most of my co-workers.
Because I hate the scattering of people in my life who like me.
Because I hate myself.

And I don't know how to write about anything other than that right now.
And it's not freeing or productive.

My mother always sends these morbid group messages to my siblings and I:
Local man stabbed, one more in hospital.
It reminds me of when we were kids
And she would try to scare us.
All the dead dirt ditches.

I have been working mostly at dropping the bad habits I picked up from
    my parents.
They are emotionally and mentally dependent on one another.
And it's suffocating for them.
And everyone around them.
And I don't know any other type of way to love someone.

I should have avoided coffee this morning.
I should have avoided *Yoshimi*.
It never sounded like a sad record to me before.

That's another projection.
And I guess I am really not working at anything.
Because I am avoiding.

--Shelby Pinkham

Writing Scars

Voices high and low surround
Whip me Flay me Chain me
Read as if unsound
They watch my every breath move

Providing the greatest weapon
Without him I'd be nothing
Alert as I step in

Soft warm hands against gagging bitter glass
Watching the laser dance about
Watching Tuesday surpass

Intense bright lights beam down
The constant burning

Scars engrave the mind
Wearing the smile she gave me
Is it really kind?
Secret whispers run by me
Your voice your friend

--Nashwa Rafiq

In the Red

Beaten to the core
Unexplainable Suffering
Success slithers through the mind
Income crawls into the corners
Neatly surrounded by the sweet spies
Estimate the dominance of green
Stingy gas hidden under class
Shiny windows stared backwards

Obeyed like a captain
Whistling calls through walls
Narrow hallways
Elevated Satisfaction celebrates
Restart

--Nashwa Rafiq

Repeated Effort

Transformation
Takes times,
Takes effort,
History in a shift,
To momentarily sit
In a murky pool of protests,
Of resistance,
Will create a path
Of blood and tears
Which are a magical
Immortality,
Forever in dusty shelves,
Accumulated weight
Of what our ancestors carried,
Walking,
Perhaps crawling,
Our simplicities
Were their luxuries,
Granted,
Times have changed,
Their crimson stained cotton
Is now our rotten
Exposed truths,
And the clues
They left behind
Are the riddles
We are now hopelessly
Trying to solve,
To be absolved
From the tragedies
We have read,
And now we
Repeatedly tread.

--Diana Ramirez

Work Shines

What is my function, you ask?
But I ask, why do I function?
I'm on a pursuit for success,
But I'm just here to impress,
We've got it all wrong,
This work thing is invented,
Imagined to be as everyone sees it,
Believe it,
Then do it,
But I've become a robot,
Automatically moving,
Incorrectly proving
My worth to who?
To me?
Or to you?
Imitation is a disintegration,
And I'm worth much more,
Feed your talents,
Tend to your seeds,
The world has engrained
A vision of failure
Which will encourage you to leave,
But you need to stay,
You're never too old to resist
Falling into a premature grave,
Dig,
Pile up the dirt,
Put in work,
To discover the gold,
To uncover your will
That your soul will not be sold
To the exploited,
Pointed
To a dead end,
But my road yields,

Curves ahead,
But I must be led
By my heart,
By my mind,
By what is right for me,
Not for anyone else,
We've allowed the hill
And the neutral gear
To feed our fear
That our passion
Should adhere
To the mundane routine,
Refuse,
Refuse,
Refuse,
Do not accuse
Anyone of leaving you in the dark,
If you decided to park,
Sit in your comfort,
Well,
Stagnation has triumphed,
Your growth requires
Movement,
Requires improvement,
All for you,
All in you,
Dig,
Keep digging,
Sweat,
Keep sweating,
Not for your grave,
Be a slave
For your dreams,
Grind,
Keep grinding,
Life is striving
To keep you alive,

To climb
Beyond,
To function
Much like the sun,
Fiercely burning,
Yearning
And begging for yet another day to shine.

--Diana Ramirez

A Cold Morn'

Bones ache and frost bites
The sun rises slowly, hidden
Fog rolls in thick as paper is thin
Wind gently roars
Hair whips side to side
The day is begun

Frozen hands fumble with keys
Doors swing slowly open
Messages are checked and sent
Now the people come

Bodies rush here and there
Lessons are taught
Smiles shine
Yet stress piles high
Minds are stretched

Help him; help her
Aid them all
Start again

Strength flags
The mind blurs
There is too much to do
Yet this is not the end

Tonight rest will come
The pillow will be a friend

The land of dreams comes forth
Journeys elapse
From beginning to end

Tomorrow everything begins again.

--Bailey Russell

Godspeed for Your Work Begun

Run here and jog there with Godspeed beneath your feet.
Be sure to turn that in and finish this and
Still put a smile on your face.

Greet the people,
Help them out,
Give a little more than all of yourself.

Sign the contract quickly but read it through.
Congratulations and welcome to the crew!

Now double fast complete the task.
The day is almost over, but not for you;
Your work is only started.

--Bailey Russell

Scritch, Scratch

Sritch, scratch, the smell of ink
The people walking by
A pungent odor of shapes and sounds
The color of the midnight sky

Scritch, scratch, the sound of parchment
A melody on the breeze
In the background a murmur drones
Like the humming of the bees.

Scritch, scratch, the flavor of words
A hero's welcome comes!
The parade a vision, nay a dream
That is the fit of drums.

Scritch, scratch, the fire's glow
Burning logs and coal
 Finished product and filled ream
My work now is whole

--Sidney Russell

Toiling, Toiling

Work or pleasure, pain or ecstasy?
Which causes me to writhe:
Labor I endure or joyous industry?
Am I weak or am I lithe?
Hearken! Hear my cry:
"I know not what I am
But still I try my to craft ply
To pass the world's exam."

Toing, toiling, working, roiling
All day and through the night,
The gears are shifting, spinning, turning;
The lamps are burning bright.
And I, yea I am here within the halls
Now writing and now breaking down the walls.

--Sidney Russell

To My Hard Working Father

Work defines a man is a saying passed down from
Generations centuries gone to the budding lives here today.
"Go out and work to provide for your family," are
Words whispered into my ear from a phantom I've rarely seen.
Where were you when I won my first spelling bee back in 2005?
Or the time my football team lost in the semifinals back in 2007?
Or when my heart was broken for the first time in 2009?

                To answer for you, you were at work, providing for the family
                    While the rest of us lived out our lives like bastards,
        Only we had a father, but didn't get the privilege of your presence.
              We were and always will be second in your life. Mom was
              Never your true love. It is and will always be your damn job.
If you could see her in the evenings sipping wine as the anguish for her
Husband who she first married drips onto the glass, maybe you would
                                            understand.

Yes it's great to provide for us, but I don't even know
You. Maybe one day you will realize you don't know
Me either. Thank you though for teaching me how to provide
For my family. I will provide them with the love you
Never showed us. That will be the work that defines me and
Make me the man you never were.
Where were you in 2017 as I read this poem?

--Mark Saso

Dirty Work

"He's just a gardener, I'm sure he doesn't even speak English,"
Bounce back and forth in the minds of strangers as they pass
Him on the sidewalk while he mows the lawn, giving the city
A taste of life that it is lacking. Everyone's too busy, caught up
In their own lives to give the man the time of day.
Thousands upon thousands pass the man giving him the same
Respect they do to the dirt. Maybe if he dressed in a suit and
Sat in an air-conditioned office, they would care to know his name
Because then he would have money and would be respected.
Instead they will pass him by and totally forget him in the three
Seconds it takes to pass him. They will never know that he
Has a daughter trying to be the first of their family to graduate college.
That is why he is pushing this lawn mower across the grass,
To bring home money to help pay for
Her schooling. Everyone continues on casting judgments
On the man. The man continues on pushing the lawn mower
With the motivation that his daughter will gain the respect he doesn't get.
He doesn't need nor does he want their respect. He will continue to work
Until his family has everything he couldn't obtain.

--Mark Saso

Condors

Condors used to feed on the moon
lifted by dream thermals to get there.
Every Yokut knew that.

And their spread wings can hide the sun—
an instant eclipse, a trick
that would make anyone look up.

But once on the ground, legendary
wings folded and put away,
they're all business,

neither brutal nor merciful:
a demo crew wielding
those bald heads like rusted claw hammers.

--Don Thompson

Yard Work

My leaf blower lifted the blackbird—
wings still spread, weightless,
floating on the loud, electric wind
almost as if it were alive.

Three or four times it flew,
but fell again, sideslipped down
like a kite with no string,
so I gave up… I had work to do,

and when the dust I raised
had settled in that other world
under the rose bushes, the ants
came back to finish theirs.

--Don Thompson

On These Streets

To Jan

I. Far From

What can possibly define
love that in a parish is far
from pulpit, altar, or pew?
It's not transparencies that
tell us who we are but such
obliqueness as can capture
a swollen vein in a person's
neck or volunteer sorrows
made obligatory. When she
brings in Sunday's supplies
for the hungry on Saturday,
diamonds dance in this their
doorway as afternoon's dust,
as she unshackles the dead
bolt and then heaves inward
the imprisoned metal gate.

II. Within Darkness

Those in need have not
yet lined up, but we can
see their halos begin to
queue in withering dark.

III. Whom

To gain entrance, each child
of God disinters what angels
lean in for; melting it down
before our eyes, he or she now
smelts one longitude and

then one latitude to this our
proleptic yet always blind
map. When our cartographers
gather, they will marvel not
at what continents we've
exhumed but at the tiny rock
on 19th Street between "B"
and "C" where angels like lap
dancers now gather to sing
only when the love we profess
grows not wings, nor martyrs,
but hatchlings, some of whom—
whom—on these streets will die,
young or old, each dismembered.

--Tim Vivian

When Memory We Inspect

I asked you then why you are so
bitter. Had no one asked you this
before? *My children*, you said,
*hate me and they don't understand
why the Alzheimer's clawing its way
through Matthew's brain is both
penance and mercy. For me, that is.*

Why, I asked, the need for penance
catastrophic, and its knees? *Isn't
such need always there?* you replied.
Yes, but.... *Don't "but" me, mister.
I don't give a shit if you are a priest.
Absolution refuses to hallow its way
through my rotten, rotting, veins. I'm
now officially old. When Matthew
dies, as soon he will, does he become
even older? Or only I? Or will he be
the renegade child I married, always
calling me into bed? Post-partum,
I fled. And I've lived here ever since.*

But with your husband's death will
you now be moving? *I'll probably
join Heather out in the desert
where there aren't any hills to be
older than. Maybe then all those
who have forgotten me will attend
me there. I hope not. When summer's
temperatures make the Devil sweat
I'll climb outside and, no longer with
church, watch pan-fried birds die and
resurrect. Matthew may be out there,
or not, but when he comes, as he will,
I'll turn the A/C on, and in that cold*

cell laugh and laugh at what we did,
and what we'll never, ever, do again.

--Tim Vivian

A Teacher's Work

when all the ugliness
of the world
is too much,
there is work,
laughter,
bright smiles,
huddled masses,
the poor with broken memories
from the dead salt sea --

send these
to me . . .
lift a lamp
beside the golden door.

knowledge is more than storied pomp
for students who whisper,
"I see" . . .
like a phoenix, rising,
yearning to be free.

-- Jana Lee Wong

A Docent's Work

among the minty eucalyptus
two monarchs in the breeze,
fly with the wind,
to protected trees.

two have fallen --
next to drought stricken death
where docents plant again
so that the mating monarchs
can fly,
locked in love's embrace.
the docent waits
for the next year's chance of survival.

"Watch your step," she whispers.

-- Jana Lee Wong

Purchase (Your Own Title)

> "Nature's first green is gold"
> --Robert Frost

At thirteen: my first paycheck cast July,
gravel road, hoe, and orders to cull
foxtails, goatheads, whatever else
had managed to sprout and seed
along that coarse mile, of which maybe
twenty yards had already been cleared.

I realized later that's how long
it had taken for at least one other
to quit for water and shade.
                          Not me.
Blistered, sweating and stinking in the sun,
I passed the first test and graduated
to unloading crates, stocking shelves, bagging
groceries for *Gifford's*, the only stop
in Springville where one could buy a carton
of eggs or six-pack of beer before making
a run up the mountains.
                        Sweeping the storeroom
I often felt my shoulder tapped, but when
I turned there was always the same nothing,
and I learned later the space was haunted
though by whom the owners couldn't say.
I wasn't scared. It just seemed like something
wanted my attention, was trying to communicate
some eternal inarticulate truth.

While overseas accents and sunglasses
postcarded their way to the sequoias . . .

While bikini-tanned locals flipflopped through
for a day spent half-drunk on the Tule . . .

While I imagined how to fill their bags
before I filled their bags, my mind grew
its own calluses as thick as any palm's.

What the fire marshal would blame on
a blown fuse reduced the aisles to blast site,
square footage in the center of town,
an opportunity for brave new builders
to resurrect fluorescent lighting.
                            Stories
of spirits no longer bore currency, but now
that I carry my own debt and struggle
to manage interest rates, I find myself
writing what the ghost had asked:

*How much of your life will you spend
selling hours, settling for seconds?*

--Matthew Woodman

Workers' Rhythm
    (after the Rufino Tamayo painting *Ritmo obrero*, 1935)

Call and response
the most efficient angle

harvest the cleanest cut
to keep the self
            sublimate
subjected
      to experience
                    time
passing

sense acclimated to the sledge
attuned to the quarry
sound the chain

tendon
      nerve
           endings

somewhere a sun might shine
somewhere a tree might leaf

all granite and grain
                  all
lift
    and release the whistle

the hands that signal
                enough
for today
      you've got tomorrow

--Matthew Woodman

About the Authors

Greg C. Bolanos is a CSUB alumni with a bachelor's degree in Theatre; he's written and produced multiple short films with the help of the CSUB Film Club and has had two plays produced locally. He plans to continue his career as a writer until the overwhelming pressure to write drives him into an early grave.

Annis Cassells is a teacher, poet, and writer who added "life coach" and "speaker" to her resume after retiring from teaching middle school. She's had poems published in several online 'zines and print anthologies. This is her second year taking part in Bakersfield's National Poetry Month Reading and Chapbook. Annis loves to travel and is always planning her next trip.

Portia Choi devotes her time promoting poetry by hosting the monthly First Friday Open Mic and publicizing events during National Poetry Month in April. She administers www.kernpoetry.com with stories and pictures of poets and poetry events. She published a chapbook of her poems *Sungsook, Korean War Poems*. She is published in in *Orpheus*, *The Asian Pacific American Journal*, *KoreAm Journal*, *A Sharp Piece of Awesome*, *Primary Point*, *Writers of Kern Anthology*, *Emeritus Voices*, *Levan Humanities Review*, and *Invisible Memoirs*. Choi previously worked in Public Health. She can be reached at portia@kernpoetry.com

Sunnee Crider is a senior in Engineering Science at CSUB with an interest in bio systems, agriculture, petroleum, and geology.

Priti Devaprakash is a 21-year-old transfer English major who studied Biology in her previous college life, still loves music, and still is trying to find a career that brings together both science and art. She is also an avid lover of animals (esp. dogs), books, philosophy, film and exploring the beauty and the tragedy of the human condition.

When she isn't writing about her family, **Erika Diaz** is a sophomore at CSUB pursuing a degree in psychology.

When he isn't fishing obscure stretches of the Kern River, **Jeff Eagan** is the Writing Center/Tutoring Coordinator and teaches English at CSUB. He loves comics, David Bowie, and eating food that will probably kill him.

Shelley Evans has been writing poetry most of her life, probably because it was her destiny, as she was named after the British poet, Percy Bysshe Shelley. Her first poem was published in 1985. In April 2016, she wrote a poem about the drought in Kern County where she resides. Shelley recited it during a formal reading at California State University - Bakersfield, and the poem was published in a chapbook for that event. Later in 2016, a poem she wrote about her memories of State College, Pennsylvania, where Shelley lived in her youth, was published in the online Town&Gown magazine in State College. Shelley typed and edited a neighbor's memoirs which were printed for his family. Recently she started a new business, Write On Poetry, composing poems for other people. Shelley is currently writing her autobiograpoem (she loves making up new words, too!) and striving toward a personal dream to publish a book of her own poetry. She works as a legal secretary in Bakersfield. She is a member of Writers of Kern, a local writing club under the California Writers Association. Shelley also enjoys traveling, Pismo Beach (any beach), reading, swimming, cooking, walking her dogs, and connecting with her friends and family.

Jack Hernandez writes in cafes and coffee shops. His caffeine inspired poems have appeared in journals like *A Sharp Piece of Awesome* and the *Anglican Theological Review*. He is currently the Director of the Norman Levan Center of the Humanities at Bakersfield College.

Anke Hodenpijl is a retired teacher. She has published in the *Phoenix Gazette*, *Denver Catholic Register*, and the *Bakersfield Californian*. Her poems have appeared in the Southern California Writer's Showcase, the "Healing Words" Anthology and the *Arizona Publishers Magazine*. She can be reached at ahodenpijl@gmail.com.

Catherine Abbey Hodges teaches English and mentors other writers at Porterville College, where her students keep her astonished. Co-coordinator of California Poets in the Schools for Tulare County, she is the author of the poetry collection *Instead of Sadness*, winner of the Barry Spacks Poetry Prize (Gunpowder Press, 2015). Her poems can be found in many journals and have been featured on *Verse Daily* and *The Writer's Almanac*. Catherine can be reached at chodges@portervillecollege.edu.

Anthony Salvador Jauregui III is a senior English and Theatre double major. A natural dilettante, Anthony enjoys writing with a deadline. His work ranges from stage to page; from lighting designs to improvised scenes to scripts of all kinds. After graduating he hopes to work as a stocker at a brick and mortar retail store and study improvisation at The Groundlings in Los Angeles.

When she isn't leaking things to the Russian government, **Emily Johnston** keeps her cover up by pretending to be a theater/history major. At the moment she is waiting further orders from Putin.

When not lifting heavy batteries for my day job, **David Kettler** enjoys writing poetry, authoring books, or building metal sculpture pieces. *One Smart Antelope*, *My Reasons in Rhyme* and *Heavy Metaling* are three of his books that are available on Amazon. He has been writing poetry since he was very young and still does when inspiration strikes.

Mateo Lara enjoys cheap wine and bad horror movies when he isn't writing poetry or being a bad person while trying to be a good person. He believes life, in general, is work, so we're constantly busy one way or another for someone or something.

His poems have appeared in *The New Engagement* and *Orpheus,* and he has published two poetry books--*Keta-Miha and Other Poems* and *La Futura Tuga*--and one chapbook--*X, Marks the Spot*--all available on Amazon. He can be reached at damnmateo@yahoo.com, for funny jokes and anything you fancy.

Rose Lester is a Marriage Family Therapist in private practice. When not seeing clients, she loves all things creative and expresses herself in many different artistic mediums. Her poems have been published in several anthologies and online websites. She volunteers for the Art for Healing program at Mercy Hospital. She can be reached at rosemft@att.net

Marit MacArthur is an associate professor of English at California State University, Bakersfield. She holds a B.A. in English and creative writing at Northwestern University, a Ph.D. in English from UC Davis, and a MFA from Warren Wilson College. Her poems and translations from the Polish have appeared in *Southwest Review, Leveler, Front Porch, Jacket2, American Poetry Review, Watershed Review, World Literature Today, Verse, ZYZZYVA, Peregrine,* the *Levan Humanities Review,* and *Airplane Reading.*

Shaina Rae Panga is a sophomore at California State University, Bakersfield majoring in Liberal Studies. She enjoys writing, feeding the wildlife at River Walk and cooking with her best friend when she has free time. You can find her volunteering and attending meetings with Sensational Sophomores, studying and/or working on assignments in the Walter W. Stiern Library, or riding her bike around campus and the surrounding areas.

Chyna Parker is a master's student who admires the art of writing; she hopes to use her passion for poetry in her career as a Licensed Marriage and Family Therapist. Chyna has been published by *Hinchas de Poesia, Orpheus,* and *One Book, One Bakersfield, One Kern.*

Shelby Pinkham is an English major, but that's really just a hobby. She is making a half-assed living as a beer snob. She has had one previous poem published, but don't bother looking for it. In her free time she is pretending to write a book.

When **Nashwa Rafiq** isn't hard at work writing strong powerful poems or expressing herself through art, she works as a CSUB ambassador. A sophomore at CSUB, she is a Liberal Studies major with a minor in art.

Diana Ramirez is a Community Outreach Coordinator at Court Appointed Special Advocate (CASA) of Kern County and recently organized "Words Come to Life," an event including art inspired by poetry, the performance of poetry, and live music.

Bailey Russell aspires to become an author and pediatrician. With her twin sister, she hopes to open a private practice that will later be expanded into a quality care clinic for people in the community who struggle financially and could not otherwise afford quality medical care. Her hobbies include reading, writing, and singing, and she can often be found studying, working at the Writing Resource Center, or spending time with her family. She intends to obtain a Ph.D. in English – either medieval literature or phonology – prior to attending medical school for her M.D., and loves reading mythology and folklore, partially as a source of inspiration for the worlds she creates in her own stories.

Sidney Russell is an aspiring pediatrician and author. In the future, she hopes to open a practice with her twin sister and eventually expand it into a quality care facility for people who cannot otherwise afford medical care. When not reading or writing, she is typically studying, working at the Writing Resource Center, or spending time with her family. Before going on to pursue her M.D., she will work toward a Ph.D. in English – medieval literature or philology, and she is always on the prowl for a good mythology book to give her ideas for her own writing.

When he is not writing, **Mark Saso** is busy attending school. He is currently a senior English major at CSU Bakersfield, coaches high school football at Centennial High School, and can be found traveling around the United States. Mark can be reached at m.saso6443@gmail.com.

Don Thompson is local fauna who languishes in other environments. He and his wife, Chris, live on her family's farm where he continues to write about the Valley as he has been doing for over fifty years. Thompson is currently the inaugural Poet Laureate of Kern County. Visit his website, *San Joaquin Ink*, at www.don-e-thompson.com.

Tim Vivian has published numerous books, article, and book reviews in his academic field of study, early Christian monasticism. He has lately turned more attention to literary efforts, publishing articles on the poetry of Denise Levertov and Rowan Williams and on the novels of Marilynne Robinson. You may reach him at tvivian@csub.edu.

Jana Lee Wong has poems appearing in *The Levan Humanities Review* and *The California Quarterly of Poetry* including "Letting Go," about the love for her daughter, "Soul Mate," a tribute to her husband, and "Time on Monk's Hill," about seeking truth and inspiration. By day, she teaches seventh and eighth graders at Standard Middle School, and by night, she teaches English at Bakersfield College. Her hobbies include traveling, swimming, hiking, cycling, and writing science fiction and poetry. She can be reached at jana.wong@bakersfieldcollege.edu.

When he is not practicing crow calls, **Matthew Woodman** teaches writing at CSUB and is the poetry editor for *Southern Pacific Review*. More of his words can be found at www.matthewwoodman.com.

Made in the USA
San Bernardino, CA
27 March 2017